Affairs of the Heart
A poetry collection

Lungani B. Malunga

ISBN-13: 978-0-620-66258-1

**Expand Your Mind
Publishers**

Durban
South Africa
www.expandyourmindpublishers.com
info@expandyourmindpublishers.com

Affairs of the Heart
A poetry collection

Lungani B. Malunga

**Expand Your Mind
Publishers**

Sometimes the heart sees
what is invisible to the
eye.

H. Jackson Brown, Jr.

ACKNOWLEDGMENTS

Firstly I would like to thank my family and friends, late and living, for teaching me the value of men, and especially for teaching me the value of respect. There are no words that can truly describe the role you have played in shaping my life. Thank you to all my social media friends for all the support all these years. A special thank you goes to Lindokuhle "Dawordplaymind" Mlangeni for introducing me to the IZIMBONGI ZENDALO poetry group and to all its members. To all the members of the Facebook poetry group of called Death of the sonnet, thank you for your encouragement.

AFFAIRS OF THE HEART

To love and to love deeply in a distance
To fall and fall in love with wind
To blow and be blown as the wind blows
To fill the inside with nothing but love
To be you with yourself but not with others

To be confused with emotions
Yet time starts to give you questions
Unseen with many words
Yet sight swallowed them all
Pure heart with challenged thoughts
Yet forward seems blank

To feel the inside as a heart beats
To feel every heart with love
To make every beat a love song in silence
I've said so many words from the heart to no one
Starved are those with an ear to listen
Starved are those with a heart to feel what I feel

I loved without telling
I felt love within
I've fallen deeply in silence
If only you knew my heart
If only you could feel my heart
If only you could hear my heart

AT LAST

Every second, minute and hour
In circles I go round and round
Like the circle my search has no end
My life is sleeping because I'm still dreaming
Feels like I'm blind because I can't see you

Like the lost soul you vanished
In my sight you were gone
In my mind you were like a written script not read
Beautiful articulated words I wrote
For you are deep within
In my eyes you were an image I can't erase

In my dreams and thoughts
I saw the inner you
I saw what the others don't know
In my sleep you were in my dreams
At last it was you in my hands

I held your fragile heart in my hands
At last you gave your heart to me
At last you gave your heart a chance to love
At last you gave it a chance to be loved

At last you are mine
At last I'm yours

BE MY REFLECTION

Let me see through your eyes,
To see what you see in me,
To see what you saw in me,
To see why you are with me

Let your eyes be my reflection
To reflect on my imperfections
Let me see deep into myself
To see what lies in there

Can you be my reflection

Be a mirror into my soul
To see if this fate could be sealed
Yes you are my reflection
You are my perfection
Again you are my imperfection

Can you be my reflection

Let your eyes be a window into your soul
For me to reflect through me
For you to see if I fit in
Let my impurity purify your soul to love
Not only I but you

Let me see myself through your eyes again

BE TOLERANT

That smile of sorrow
That laughter of anger
That kiss that sooths the mood
How soon did we mess our life

You looked at my eyes and smiled
Yet in deep you begged to differ
In my face you lied and laughed
In yours you shared no light

Wounded heart that bared scars of yesterday's torture
Scars that bleeds to new life
Wounds that brushed on
To new life you showed anger

Unstable source gave birth to us
Negligence ran deep within
How soon we lost hope
Look at me and tell the truth

Be tolerant to others and you'll be loved for life

BE WHO YOU ARE

Time and time again things change
Even when times change be still
Through gale force winds
And through towering weathers

Be who you are

When life weighs you down
And when earth calls you down
Tall you stand with courage
Like a soldier on you march

When your name changes,
"Repeatedly"
When the earth shows you no smile
With your heart and soul mutilated
Gnarled emotions in a wild empty dome

Be still and be who you are

Wrecked image as they wish you to be
Damsel as they call you to dread
In the ponderously league of life
Regally impediments taken strength
Be strong when they call you to harlot

With the dwindling shaft to night
When you feel your eyes lolling to lashes
When sudden gales tremor you to natural unconsciousness
With gaze abstracted notions in your sleep
As you woke up in twilight

A new life begin

Walk tall and stain no life
Stay strong when they weather ye down
Be who you are no camouflage
With naked eye they shall see

BLOOD RUSH

In a distance I swallow movements
From far my sight I stare
Skewed vision as I danced to death
Blood rushing I stood robotically
Stare fish eyes I stood muted

Death danced erotically
Death embodies the embedded lust
Like gush my mood rose
Simultaneously you pleaded the same
We shared a plate on a fatal land

Stolen joy gave birth to a death bed
Instant emotions took over
Rational life blinded by blood rush
Viral shield hasten from sight
It was joy for awhile

Now my life is wrecked
Stuck in a vast whole with plague
This woe chartered mine
Foregone is mine as I swallow my pride to rest
In this latter of life I leave you to reason

CAGED

Being prisoned for no reason
Locked up in this small cage
Wonder where you are
Why won't you tell the truth

I know it wasn't your choice
But remember I was your choice
Remember it was me and you
Those passionate moments we shared

Deep inside I'm caged
I'm sorry they asked you to choose
Wonder what your heart feels
Wonder how it feels to love from distance

Closed walls suffocating my existence
As I pleaded my innocence
They changed mine to convict
They changed me for your lies
But I'm guilty of loving

Your words I loved
Your smile I crave
Your truth I seek

Everyday feels like a year
I sleep with my eyes open
As danger lives around me
Freedom to me is a dream
As I lost my private time

I chose to be with you
We chose to be together

But you let them in
You never told me a lie
Why now, remember us

Look as I reach for your heart
Come release me from this cage
Bring back my freedom
Bring me back to us

DEAD BEFORE TIME

Just as the wind blows
As the eye glanced
As my hands reach for you

Just as the new born
Fresh from the womb
Just as I start to rejoice
As you start to really breath
As life begins to emerge

Like ice you melted away
Just as my heart began to feel
As I started to see openly
As we started to blend

Just before we fell in love
As things started to make sense
As my heart started to take the first step
You vanished like smoke in the air
Your soul was lost to us

You were dead before my time
You perished in the palm of my hand
Now I tear myself to sleep
As you were dead before time

DEAR DISTANCE

Oh fuck distance, as you limit my feelings to words without actions,
But fuck you'll never win
Ice cold outside on my God given wheels turning kilometres to metres
Day and night became the same with my beloved on my mind
And my heart yearning to feel yours close

Dear distance, to me you are just an obstacle
A hurdle a steep slope a dam
Ooh distance you are nothing that I can fear
You won many battles but not mine

Dear distance, today I fold you like a blanket to fit my arms
As I want to feel my beloved in arms reach

Dear distance, to me you are nothing but a motivation that keeps me
running for love,
You give a me chance to put a picture in my imagination

DEAR YOU

I write to you with the hope
That you'll read this and answer back
I write to you this with the hope
That you'll feel those words
And let them sink into your nature
You are what's on my mind all day
You are that melody that rings in my heart day and night

Dear you
You are that mental picture stuck in my head
That song that my heart dances to
The source that gives me joy
As you give joy to my heart with your warmth

Dear you
The light in my darkness
The reality in my dreams
The air in my breathe
The heart of my soul

Dear you
The freedom to my struggle
I write to you to feel my feel
For your eyes to feast into my heart
I write for your soul to live in my thoughts
I write to paint a mental picture in your mind

Dear you
I write to you to make you understand
The importance your words have in the next chapter
As you take your pen be sure you heard
My words and what my heart feels

DEFINE LOVE

Truth is I can't define love
Strangely I've been thinking
Yet love remains thinking
The sun set on those cold early mornings
That tormented my soul to define love for I am lost
Wondering years longing to honour love
My effort seems to go to waste
How soon will the questions be answered
Bloom as the day slowly totters to sleep
That vast silence of uncertainty creeps in
Pondering beats seeks to find its rhyme
As the count starts to lose it sequence
I mumble as no words speaks to what I desire
Forever I shall strive to define what love is

FORBIDDEN TRUTH

I spoke to the death like the living, but the living was I not
Though yet their words lived through me.
The dead smiled upon my eyes as I awake to see the forbidden truth
Through the valley of death my eyes saw life like a new born who tasted
Life for the first time.

Songs sung with sweet harmonies gave birth to joy
As I summon my soul to the almighty
Sweet joy with a smile as we glance to life with simultaneous thoughts
So deep with heavy beats as our heart pounds with joy

Your tongue smeared words to endure life
Yet words probe the endurance perceived
Sound reverted the unseen to the specific
I foresaw joy with the endless within as life preceded I to love

No now no tomorrow yet your words lived forever
As eyes open I saw sorrow like a star but it never smiled nor shone
Forsaken are those whose ears heard nothing, whose eyes saw
Something, whose heart felt no guilt, whose actions disappeared
With love.
Love lost never found left a chest with a hole as I open my eyes
To see the forbidden truth.

FOREVER NEVER DIES

Forever never dies
Forever will never last
Family you never loved
Friends I never had
Confused as I ever been
You will never be
So why should we be

At your presence I was yours
At your absence I was still yours
But still we will never be;

I gave it all with no return
You took it all with no remorse
Yet love to you remained unfulfilled
I knew together will never last

Patient was I as I waited for my love to be returned
Like a tamed horse I remain grounded
But you showed no love
Yet for you silence broke
But still family you never loved

In you life was a blessing
You were my everything
I gave you everything
Confused as I have ever been
In your thoughts I became a reality

Now I remain crippled as my heart
Sees no reason to love.
For the one I love left me frozen in love
With the future that has no us but I

They say forever never dies;
But you and I will never be

FORGIVE ME

Forgive me my words
Forgive me my actions
It wasn't my intention
I didn't know

It wasn't because you meant nothing
It's not that you didn't play your part
It's not that we didn't show love
Your part you played
It was I who didn't participate

Forgive me my intolerance
I showed you no trust
I gave you no reason to trust
I made your heart bleed
In my presence you cried
But still I showed you no companion

In the land of we you stood alone
Forgive me your unhappiness
As I seek to mend your broken heart
In the flight of time I hope you forgive me

It's not that I meant it
It's not that I wanted to
It's not that I wished for it
It's not that you didn't prove your love
It's because I wasn't ready to love

I now commit myself to thee
For life I owe it to you
If you find it in your heart to forgive me
I'll be in you debt for life

HARDSHIPS

It's hard to stay in love when the one you in love with pushes you away,
When your heart gives and gets nothing in return
When all you get is silent conversation

I keep banging on the door but still silence speaks loud
Is it that my knocks fell on deaf ears
Is my cry not loud enough to be heard in yours
Mine is in search of a path to yours
It seeks to share its tears with yours
To cuddle yours to its warmth

How I feel as you pull apart its needs
Engraved pain stuck within
As it feels the embedded love of men
As the heart seeks to find its missing link
The link to your heart

Again it's hard to be in love, when the one you love pushes you away
When your heart gives and gets nothing in return,
When all you get is silent conversation

When the one that melts your heart shows no emotions
When the one you love can't be within your arms reach
When your heart lives in wonderland

HEART THAT LOVES

An angel in my eyes
Joy in my heart
In my mind you were mine
Like a summer day your smile was so bright
I loved you from a distance
In my eyes I saw a saint

I loved you wholeheartedly
Time we shared together I'll cherish
Love you gave to me I never deserved
Joy we had was priceless
Laughter we shared under the moonlight as the stars moved
To move my heart, yet yours was mine and mine was yours

You trusted me with your life, in your life I brought sorrow
Upon your heart.
Oh that heart that loved
oh heart that loved now filled with anger
You once loved, I once loved.
That heart that once loved now possesses more hate and anger
Than love.
You once wished me life but now that life you want to take

I once was a saint
I once was trustworthy, faithful, honest and loving.
Now I've turned into a monster
I crushed every good you brought In my life.
I've destroyed all that we built, in all of this;
I regret that I ever broke your heart.
Now what I wish for is that you could forgive
My stupidity, that you could forgive my blindness that caused me to
Crush what was given to me with love.
I wish you don't regret the time we spent together

I wish you'll not only see the man I've become but see
The man I was and see the man I can be in the future.

I regret that I ever broke your heart
I regret the pain and bruises I caused you and those tears you cried
But one thing I don't regret is "LOVING YOU"
And I thank you for that heart that loved.

HEARTS SECRETS

Far from a distance
Sticky thighs as my eyes glanced
Her looks define beauty
We talked without love
Her bold voice tendered my heart

Like my life was on rewind
I see the same everyday
They say nothing is impossible
It is possible that you might be
I say without words we could be

I silenced the unspoken words as my heart spits
More desires to bridge limited thoughts
Like the forbidden truth my words were tamed
If only eyes could tell maybe you'll see
My thoughts gave me a smile
As you are in them

Oh how I wish me and you
Thoughts twisted ideas in different stresses
Words gave birth to nothing
Yours may not feel like I
Yet your smile remains the same
Like we were not meant to be we don't see
A new day shall conceive love

I bow before your heart and whisper
Seeds to grow and bloom
I chant love to plead with thee
Songs of love plodded my mind
Yet tomorrow is unseen to the presence
Let no thoughts nor words stop tomorrow

HELLO AGAIN

Again those feelings lost in the process of love
Again those tears drop from the gorgeous eyes were wasted because
we were not equally committed
Those broken hearts crying for love lost in the mist of lust

We didn't see it committing
We thought all was good
Yet all now is lost
All we have are regrets

Now my heart pleads for love
As I beg for your forgiveness
Like a fool I let temptations keep me from you
I was taken by early morning mist before the sun shines
Now it's day time I can see clearly
It's you I want

My heart craves to be yours again
It craves to see your smile again
It seeks to be in your warmth
It seeks a chance to say hello again

HER SMILE

She smiles to take away my day's frustration
Her voice sings forever in my ears
Her coolness brings me closer
Wonder if she can see my tears
As she smiles just to see me smile

She intrigued my heart with love
To love and love her more
She smiles just for me
To show she approves
As I take her hand and hold it for awhile

She never made me question her smile
Oh she, she showed me her inner beauty
Ooh she is the beat that beats in my heart always
Her smile, her smile completes every word she says
From the first time we met
She smiled as to say you're welcomed in world
In her world I live to see her smile

HOW COULD

I feel lost, lost in the path of love
Lost in the journey of life
Sideways I go with no direction
No Idea of my ideal way forward
Forward I go searching for you
Yes forward, backwards and
Sideways I go but seem to be
In the same position that I was in

How soon can we meet
How long should I wait
Where can we meet

In your presence I felt lonely
I've searched for you and I've failed
Your heart I'm a failure
To your heart I'm nothing
Yet to mine you mean the world

So I ask, how could this be
How could the one in my heart
Feel me no more
How can I be in love with wind
So I ask will mine ever heal
Will mine be able to live alone

I was yours and you were mine
What changed
How could yours forget so easily
How could you leave mine hanging
Why did you let us break

HOW DO I TELL HER

You come my way with the remedy of my soul
I look to thee with the sense that you'll see me
I smile with the sight of your face as you pass me by
My heart starts to feel for you then I fall for you

With your eyes looking my way
Mine at yours
Thoughts running through my mind
As I ask if you feel how I feel.
Fear as my action shows less to prove how I feel
Fear as I feel time slowly leaving me
With no option but to tell you how I feel.

Thoughts as I seek the ways to find thee.
How do I tell thee of my love
I see her with the eyes of my heart
As my heart tells me to tell you how I feel
Guilty am I as I fail to honour my heart's desire

How do I tell her that she is the one,
One that my heart desires
Please tell me how do I tell her.

I'M SORRY

Silence spoke loud as her heart drowns in those tears
His guilt pleaded with open arms as her heart beats to his
Her face drowns deep as tears poured
Regrets thickened deep as he saw her heart broke
Tears never stopped but engraved in her faced
His actions never stopped but wished for change
Into yesterday he wished to change his ways
To him I asked for your love
Yet to your love I've failed
Tear me not for this pain is not for me but my actions
Tear me not for her tears are of me

Into her silence her tears spread more words
Her heart shredded by my own
Different zones scattering rain on her beautiful face
My heart pounded with the hate of self
How soon did we meet
Yet we broke
My heart bruised and pouring tears of regrets

Into yesterday a different song could've been sung
Different strings could've strung
In her cry her voice was melodious but sad
Into yesterday questions I asked
Bitter answers I find
So soon we came to a halt
Our love tunnel came to face
Again questions I ask
How could this be

Gentle is her voice and touch
That I so deeply crave to hear and feel
Sweet are her lips

That I so deeply crave to kiss and taste
Her artistic smile that tickles my spine
Her body that gently sways to steal my sight so still
I still swoon about you

No day passes but I miss you
I'm sorry is the song I sing to you
I'll love you forever and live in it
In your heart I hope forgiveness can be conceived
I shall wait for you to give my life sight
Until forever I shall wait and live for you

I THOUGHT MORE WAS TO COME

Wonders of the day
Through time I waited
Through laughter I waited
For long you knew my cry

I perceived through time
You gave no sign to resist
I swallowed my fright and spoke
I felt yours in my arms as you hugged
And kissed me goodbye
Speechless was I to say the same

Through time things didn't change
Yet again I swallowed my fright
In the end I got the same
I swore tomorrow I will change
Yet tomorrow stared me in the face

I thought more was to come
From those goodbye hugs and kisses
I wished for more
From those moments with eyes I thought
Things will grow
From no response I thought you needed more time
I foresaw between us love
Yet into tomorrow I saw wrong
I thought more was to come

I WISH I KNEW

The seductive eyes of loneliness
Licking your lips to lure me to your prison
As your body replicates that of a snake
Glued was mine to yours

If only I knew it was all pretence
As you smothered me with weird emotions
I believed in love at first sight
My first became my sentence

To life mine was changed
As I wonder through life with death
I knew nothing but you did
You showed me everything

Guess I was fooled by my naked eyes
You had no one as you took my innocence
As you crucified my soul for life
How could this beauty be tainted

If I know I wouldn't fall for you
I wouldn't resign myself to your death bed
I wouldn't deny my eye sight
I wouldn't commit my innocence

IF ONLY I COULD BE THERE

Night and day I cry
Day and night you cried
Tears I cried you cried
Heads shared us some thoughts
Time shared me with your love
Space showered me with your heart
If only I could be there

Let it be that I'm yours
Let no space separate me and you
Let no space separate our thoughts
Let no one be between us
May it be you in my dreams

Let my heart be the one you desire
Let my hands be the one that hold you close
Even on your cry,
Let me be the one that dries your tears
Let nothing put any doubts in your mind
Let our dreams and wishes run its course
Let love bring us even more closer

As my body craves for your touch
Only thoughts covers distance
But with thoughts I touched you gently
With thoughts my mind caress my heart to sleep
In my dreams came a wish
If only I could be there
To assure you my love
To fill my heart with love

IF ROLES WERE REVERSED

At first I thought it was fate
In the beginning I saw the light
In your eyes I saw the fire
In my heart yes it was burning
When I looked at yours
My world was complete

They say time tells
This time it showed me the impossible
With a blink of an eye things changed
You left without a word
Stranded was my soul
Guess someone swept your heart away

Remember that it was you
It was you who said we should make this promise
When we promise not to be apart
You taught me not to look at other girls
Now please tell me whose going to unteach me that
Who has to let go of what he thought was his

Tell me how do I tell my heart to let go
Please tell me how do you undo years of work
I wonder if roles were reversed how would you feel
Tell me how will your heart feel
How will you erase all those memories
Tell me how will you fold that chapter
Just knew in my heart this has an open ending

LET ME LIVE THIS LIFE AND GET OVER IT

Deep within I know my fate
Long before I came to face to face with my fate
My destiny and I met before time
Now I'm a friend with your enemy

While they try hard not to get you
I try so hard to live with you
I met you in a beautiful body
Now that body is lost to earth
And I know I'll soon be

While they cry for my fatal life style
I try to put it to speed
I met my fate and missed the date
Now I live not to see the date
Now I live not to see the next
If it should come I'll be happy

They try to make mine long
They're on their knees begging
And I'm on mine doing the same
But we beg for a different outcome
Hope you answer mine first

Now see I'm emaciated
So I ask him
Not to make mine longer
And I ask them
Not to control my actions
I ask them to
Let me live this life and get over it

LIKE THE UNCUT

Like the uncut you were raw
As I tasted blood in that meal
Fresh in that clean plate
I swallowed it with pride

Phenomenal are your thoughts
As you shared them with ease
Reminding me of my being
True as you were
I wonder where mine went

You are the uncut
You shine on your originality
Clean as a new born
Yet you shared a vision of life
Like a prophet you knew my next chapter

I tasted life in your words
Your words gave sight to the light
Blinded by the inner most fear
You were like the first step of a new born
As I took mine to new life

You were like the uncut your words were raw
Your words and voice spoke to me
In deep your words stood
In my heart yours engraved itself
I now shall live upon its roots

MIRACLE ON THE WALL

Little miracle on the wall
As I glance to the sun's rays
Sleepy eyes stare from a distance
Silent as mine could be
In my eyes you stand

Art painted deep within
Colours bright emotions
Thoughts wrote to heart
In deep the heart felt
Clear crystal eyes I stare

In memory its love we shared
But for now its distance we share
With shared moments drew me in
Still is your love standing

Time folds as love pride floats
Lapse are theirs as we share
Distance apart folds on the wall
Sun rays enlighten my sights
Love moments last through time

Little miracle on the wall
I stare to wall for time.

MY CONDOLANCES

Seemingly lost emotions
In this reel of life
As death roars to nature
When laughter swells
And joy balloons to earth
Wane all to silent death

Pouring sea in those grim faces
To a love letter death is sent
To heart it reads sadness
My condolences

My condolences as I gain your loss
As you whimper in the dark
Gaze to the future's brow
Sing to it my unhappiness
Clubbed is my heart to lose

The one I love is no more
The spirit vanished like frost in the sun
Lost is the touch of laughter
As death sings to me

My condolences
To the heart that lost
To the soul filled with despair
To the life that shares nothing but pain

I pledge nothing but my condolences

MY HEART

In search of a place to put mine
On the lookout for prosperity
My hide out seems to be in hiding
Searching for the unknown
On the road with bruises

I'm in search to find my comfort
On the lookout for eternity
In deep sinking with loneliness
With my trembling fear

In search to find my shepherd
To find a place with direction
To find shape to align mine

In search to find courage
To find my mate
In search to find the light
In search to find safety for my heart

NO MAN IS AN ISLAND

Alone I stood in the dark wondering
Like an owl the dark gave me strength
Like the blind man I couldn't see the light
In the dark I swam deep into loneliness

Like an eagle I fly alone
On my level I shared no smile
Without fear I showed my pride
Yet my pride led me deep
In deep I swam in the dark

Voices from side to side speaks
From ear to ear voices speak
"No man is an island"
Like a deaf man I didn't hear
Discarded was your affection towards me

Vigorously your best you tried
Like a song on my mind you kept on repeating
"No man is an island"
Like a fool I didn't listen
Stuck is my life
With no one to lean on

NO REGRET

Pounding heart with no regret
Heavy head filled with my thoughts
Deep in my thoughts I wonder, wondering
About I, for I didn't know thee
Pounding heart as I see thee with the eyes
Of sorrow as she passes by with no words spoken
for I had so many to say

Time has passed by with you thinking
that I was just fooling around
But hey it wasn't the right time for me
To make my move, for I have respect for thee
Deep In my thoughts you were the one who kept me strong
When things went bad on my side
Just the thought that you're waiting for me
Gave me the will to prosper

But now that is lost just because I gave it time
It wasn't my choosing but Gods choosing
Pounding heart filled with regrets as I ask for your forgiveness
With open thoughts I swallowed your cry
And thoughts gave birth to forgiveness
Regret me no more as time has given birth to us to share our cry

Thoughts bared in tongue with the presence of your heart
For your heart has given me no regrets.
Swallowed is my lost with one thought on my mind
My heart beat with no regrets
Time came for us to live life with no regrets.

REJECTION

Sadness is the title of my life
Tears like showers in my daily routine
Raw cries like a wild king as he marks his place
Yet mine has no place
I'm out of place like a bat in the dark

I came to thee with a heart
Yet I return with a hole
I came to you for a hand
I returned with a broken heart
I came to you to hear my cry
Yet you saw a need to laugh at my face

You are what pain is, you are what hate is
The pain I've suffered is because of you
The tears I've cried it's all you
The sadness in my face yes that's you
The shame in my life that's all because of you

Now I see no reason to share a smile
Now I have a heart that bleeds no love
Now I see me and see no life
Now I see a chance you never gave me
I hear words you said about me
I hear words you said in my face
And I wonder what did I do to deserve this

Who am I no one wishes to know
Who I'll be no one seems to care
I live in the land of no acceptance
I've learnt to live with rejection
I've learn to accept my none acceptance
For rejection is my name.

REMIND ME, WHAT I'VE JUST SAID

Forgetting is my problem
So don't mind me if I ask you
To remind me what I just said.

It is not that you are of no importance to my memory
It is not that I'm lying but to remind me of my words
It is not that I'm stupid but the fact that I love to hear you speak
It is not that I've forgotten but that I love to hear you say
Those words
So please remind me what I just said.

I smiled without fear
Yet I had a race with my heart
You make my heart dance to the beat of your heart
I love you like no other
It is not that I forgot
But that I love to hear your voice.
Please remind me what I just told you

It's not that I forgot
But it's that I want to hear if you were
Listening to my words
Now my wish is for you to feel the same
My wish is for you to be mine and mine to be yours forever
I wish for you to take my hand and tell me how you feel
Tell me you feel the same way
Now please remind me what I just said
It's not that I forgot but that I want to hear your voice in my ear.

SEALED WITH A TEAR

My heart bleeds with the sight of your words
As I seek to find Inspiration
Forgive my heart for it has been deceived
By that my eyes saw
Forgiveness not of you but from you made it so
Hard to ignore what I saw

I write to you for your forgiveness
Not that I did you bad
But because we did it bad
Brief as it was but our heart will explain.
Sweet as it tasted our heart remains tested
See me now, now you don't, it's how we were

Prints in my heart as I try to clean the dirt
For my heart I hope to see you more
Write to me as your thought I seek to hear
I write to you for your heart I seek to move
Smile as I seal this letter with a tear.

SHE HAD MINE

She had my heart long before I knew
Her impurity purified my soul to rest
Still I stood awaiting
That glimpse of hope
Hope that tomorrow blossoms
Like the summer rose
That blossomed through winter colds
Strong was her stature
That soaked my love into her
My heart stood no chance against her charm
As she blushed just to see my firmament side
Gazing winds that blew my heart away
As my soul slowly totters her way
She had mine in an instant.

SHE

Pure is how I view thee
Silence made me wonder
As I reminisce with nothing but your eyes
As I stole that moment for a second

Fair like the sun in the sky
Muted is our conversation
As I look to thee stunned
Secretly I stole your smile
As your body calls

Now I wonder what's in your mind
As she spoke I was moved
She moved my thoughts
As yesterday became blurred

I took to now and dreamt
Yet circumstances differ
Few words I could speak
If only you can lend me your ear

Far from the end
Yet I foresaw this like a dream
A dream in the thy silent self
Faraway visions
And silent words mumbled

SO CLOSE BUT YET SO FAR

Like a traveller I've walked with a chip on my shoulder
I've seen not only glamour but glitter
They say heaven on earth
Its heaven on my hands
With nobody to take me there but myself
I strive not only to live but stay there

I've been in the tenderness of your arms
I've shared space and time with you
I felt your lips on mine like a dream
I held you in my arms and felt your heart beat
We shared laughter and joy together

If only you knew how I feel
If only you could read my eyes when I look at you
If only you knew how hard it's been to me
If I could tell you what's inside my heart
If my actions can't show you enough
No much words can explain more

I'm so close yet too far for you to understand
I have your heart and you have mine
We connected yet we separated
We speak of one another's love
I'm stuck with the wonders of what could be
Soo close to your heart but far
You see me as a friend
Yet to me you are more
It's a silent cry sent to you
I'm close yet so far

BLESSING AND CURSE

On the edge of glory
Stimulated by fame
Living the life of glitter
Feeling blessed by success

Motion pictures giving me the nod
Society preaching my name
My name beating through every drum
Fame the story of my life

Now I'm living your life
Your life I dreamt off
Now I'm boxed up with flashes
Guess this is what I chose

Feeling prisoned by a dream
Losing my freedom for fame
Printed words rule my ways
Everyone counting my actions

Loosing friends for fame
Loving life without space
Suffocated by fame
I found my dream and lost my life

THOSE WORDS

Please just don't say anything
Say no more as my soul can't take no more
Be mute as those words hurt my feelings
After all this time you choose to say those words
At this hour
How could you

With your words you just hurt my soul
The pain I feel now through your words
Never have I felt like this before
So many moments together but you just swept it all
With two words.

How could you let me fall like that
The time we spent together is gone just like that
How could you be so sure that it's for the best
How I hate those words now just because you
Said them to me
How could you say those words

Words I hate to hear now I hate to write
Please don't say those words, don't write me those words.

TOMORROW

Like the times of oppression my life is a riot
Fighting day and night to see tomorrow
Yet tomorrow showed me nothing but tears
Fears of yesterday's pain lives through days of anger

Like the lost soul my path is lost
Like Jesus seekers come be my saviour
Come take away this pain within
Come take away this pain of wonder

Like a blind man I can't see my tomorrow
Please remind me of my yesterday
As I struggle to juggle my memory into remembrance
Like a dog can you be my guide
Show me tomorrow as I'm stuck in yesterday

Let my tomorrow be written with a clear mind
Let my heart be pure
Let tomorrow be strong for life

UFAZED WORDS

Ideas engraved deep in my mind for a life time
Yet no life lived through them
Who was I before these ideas no one could tell
For my words shared no light to the above
Suffocated words with no blinks
Yet again my ideas glimmer hope

I spoke the forsaken language like a forbidden child
For my mind to be heard
I'll forever not hold the truth but I'll speak it
Fuck those whose ears close when my voice chants
Truth forever prevail to unveil the limits of your thoughts

I'll forever not bow to the devil's mind
I'll forever hold my own in the womb of the cross
I'll my spit to mute words to be heard
As I gazed at the devil's gate and gave it my back

Silence broke free and we shall forever speak the truth fully
My words will stand tall to be real with words and my thoughts
My ideas and words will face silence no more
As I swore truthfully in my words

I will not forget the meaning of my words
I'll speak success in the dead minds
I'll speak life in the dead souls
I'll speak sorrow no more but joy
As I'll forever hold the light of life in my hands
And the glimmer of hope in my words.

WAITING IN VEIN

You said you needed time
To my foolishness I gave you time
You said you needed some space
I try to ask why, you didn't tell
With my heart torn apart I agreed
Yet to your greed you still ask for more
With nothing to give yet you devoured everything
You took from the hand that fed your soul

They told me, I didn't listen
They warned me but I trusted you
I gave you time
Time to think of what you want in life
What you wish to gain
I gave you space
With that space you created more
You chose to be more ignorant
Through your ignorance you left us separated
I wonder if my pain feeds your soul
As you inflict more and more as days go by

Am I waiting in vein
They say I have eyes yet I can't see
But I say you have a heart yet you do not feel
You have denied yourself love for your past brutality

Don't let your past be immortal to your heart
Allow yourself to be loved not used
Allow yourself to feel
I know you told yourself not to trust men again
But not all things are the same, neither are men

Not all women have the strength to turn back, but you can

Just believe, feel and trust in yourself
Let your heart and mind work and not be told
What to think or feel

Now again I ask
Did I give you time and space in vane
Did you find your strength to be true to yourself

WAS IT ALL A DREAM

Nice shiny day,
Green leaves, slow breeze
Beautiful thoughts floating in my mind
Sweet gentle music
Singing songs of nature
Clear blue skies
As clouds paved the way for me

Face to face I come to you
Sins of the past came before me
With a heavy head I bow before thee
On my knees I ask for forgiveness
With time running out of my life
As I felt tears within my heart
But my eyes draw blank

Fear within my soul, thoughts turned my body to ice
As I feel my body with funny moves
Lost are the times I had with you
Lost are the times I had with you
Lost are the ideas I had for you
With my eyes closed I saw you
I see you far away from my reach
Fast beats as my heart beats
The beat of lost
Eyes open as I see you
Then I ask
Was it all a dream?

WE ARE WHAT LOVE IS

Forever we strike a pose as a couple with no regret
Together we grow like a tree that drinks from the fountain of love
We share smiles and laughter like its comedy nights
We forever in each other's arms like first time lovers

People spoke otherwise to us
Yet like two opposite magnetic fields we are attracted to each other
We grew strong with every word

We are what love is
We are what many wish to be
We argue to make it right
We fight to take flight
Our love for one another is unmatched
We bring hope to life

We are what love is
If forever ever existed
Then forever will be you and I
Together you and I, true love was defined
Faith prevails life among us
Yet love paved a way to life
Light before sunshine gave us life
Forever are we as we are together for life.

WHY YOU LET US BROKE

A journey to your heart has caused me so many sour moments in my
heart
My heart has turned to wonder or was it manipulated by your beauty
into falling for you
How could something so beautiful and so innocent as you do such a
cruel thing to someone
They say the world is a cruel place to live in, now I see why
How could you break such a wonderful joy
If it wasn't so, then why did you let me into your heart

When we were together we only cried with joy
But now it's no more we but I
What happened to us
I loved you with all my heart
I gave you all I had

Together we were everything
Alone I'm nothing filled with loneliness
Craving to feel your touch
In my dark days all I hear is your voice
Your voice when you said it's over

Without any explanation our journey ended
Our joy vanished, us became I
I wonder what would I be without you
Wonder why you had to leave
Wonder why you let us broke

The pain of yesterday's pain broke loose
As tears galloped down my face
Guess I wasn't man enough for you
Hope you find what you looking for
Still wonder why you let us broke

WINDS OF LOVE

Like a girl I love you came my way
In a bunch of heads you chose mine
With your presence my coat ripped open
Your breeze stole my attention
Silenced as trees danced to your song

With no words your eyes smiled
With your smile it was full moon in my eyes
Plain with no stain you stood
Visions of tomorrow conceive joy
In that moment it was wonderland

Joy embedded deep swallowed grief
I hope we can marry this moment
And make it an everlasting moment
As we hold hands and never let go
Wish the only time we let go is
When one of us forgets to breath

You'll forever be in mine I hope you feel the same.

YOU ARE

Like the river that flows
Like the stars in the sky
The light in the dark
You shine like full moon in the sky
You are
The memory deep within
A thought crafted within
A feeling engraved within

With a smile I stare thinking
With a thought on my mind
I glance and saw my future
Like a dream you were there

In reality you are part of my dream
I feel you touching the inner me
Your heart in sync with mine
Mechanically we chained together

Pinch me twice and I woke up
You were in my dream
You are my dream
You are the future in my present

YOU MAYBE GONE BUT YOU'LL NEVER BE FORGOTTEN

I need no reason to cry
I remember you like yesterday
That smile on your face
That touch that tickles my skin
Those days and nights we shared
Those promises we made

I see you now as my yesterday
Not my now neither my tomorrow
How can this be so soon
Your love still crafted deep
With new starts new ways
But you still in my mind

You left me without any goodbyes
Sadness in my soul painted the everlasting one
You left me scarred for life
With my new, new ways I hope to find true peace
When eyes collide I still remember you
We may not be together but just know that
You may be gone but you'll never be forgotten
I still think about you.

YOU MAYBE GONE BUT YOU'LL NEVER BE FORGOTTEN 2

You left me in an instant
You left in a blink of an eye
I thought more was to come
But you left me to surprised
I thought more was to come

You taught me life
Yet I saw yours fading in my eyes
You gave me strength
Yet mine was not enough to keep yours
You gave me a voice
But yours was never there to say those last words
You gave us love that does not choose

In my heart only few things stay
In my regret you are never one
Upon your life I bow myself
And wish you eternity and hope you know that
You may be gone but you'll never be forgotten
In my heart you'll forever be there
I'll forever have you in my thoughts
I'll forever share a smile in your name

ABOUT THE AUTHOR

LUNGANI .B. MALUNGA was born and raised in the southern rural part of KwaZulu Natal. He started writing as a hobby in high school. Lungani has always been fascinated by poetry and got introduced to a poetry group in in Lamontville called Bleeding Pen. His writing is inspired by life. Affairs of the heart is the reflection of life and is his first published poetry collection.

www.ingramcontent.com/pod-product-compliance
Lightning Source LLC
Chambersburg PA
CBHW071849020426
42331CB00007B/1930